BEARS

BY MARTIN SCHWABACHER

BENCHMARK BOOKS

MARSHALL CAVENDISH
NEW YORK

Series Consultant:
James Doherty
General Curator
The Bronx Zoo, New York

Benchmark Books
Marshall Cavendish Corporation
99 White Plains Road
Tarrytown, NY 10591-9001

Library of Congress Cataloging-in-Publication Data
Schwabacher, Martin.
Bears / by Martin Schwabacher.
p. cm. – (Animals, animals)
Includes bibliographical references and index (p. 48)
Summary: Describes the eight different kinds of bears that live around the world, including their physical characteris-
tics, their food and how they find it, their reproductive behavior, and the threats from human beings to their survival.
ISBN 0-7614-1169-0
1.Bears—Juvenile literature. [1. Bears.] I. Title. II. Series.
QL 737.C27   S377   2000
599.78—dc21   00-027638

Cover photo: *Animals, Animals* / Johnny Johnson

All photographs are used by permission and through the courtesy of *Animals, Animals*: Norbert Rosing: 4, 14, 32 (top), 35;
Tom Edwards: 7; Barbara Von Hoffman: 8; Lynn Stone: 10 (left), 27, 39; Charles Palek: 10 (right); Mark Stouffer: 13; Maresa
Pryor: 15; S. Osolinski: 16; Phyllis Greenberg: 20, 26; Johnny Johnson: 23; Howie Garber: 24; Bates Littlehales: 29; Stouffer
Prod.: 31, 38; Leonard Lee Rue II: 32 (bottom); Ray Richardson: 34; Shane Moore: 36; Richard Sobol: 40.

Printed in the United States of America

1 3 5 6 4 2

C O N T E N T S

1

INTRODUCING BEARS

In Africa, the lion is the "king of beasts." But in North America and Asia, another beast rules: the bear. Lions are the biggest cat, while bears are more closely related to the dog family. Though the smallest, the sun bear, is barely bigger than a pet dog, the biggest—the polar bear—can weigh up to a *ton*.

Bears may look slow-moving and even lazy, but their loose skin and baggy layer of fat hide an awesome power. Some bears can run forty miles (sixty kilometers) per hour—fast enough to catch a running horse. Their mighty

POLAR BEARS PRACTICE THEIR HUNTING SKILLS BY PLAY-FIGHTING.

jaws can snap right through a tree trunk.

Most bears have short legs, thick fur, small, round ears, and short, stubby tails. Their long claws are great for climbing trees and digging holes, and they have an excellent sense of smell. If you met a black bear, it could tell your age, sex, and even what you ate for lunch, just by smelling you.

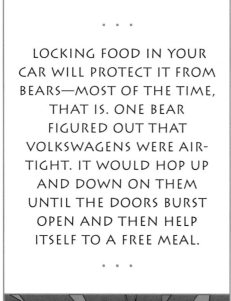

THE POLAR BEAR IS THE LARGEST MEMBER OF THE BEAR FAMILY. THE SMALLEST, THE SUN BEAR, IS THE SIZE OF A LARGE DOG.

SECOND IN SIZE ONLY TO POLAR BEARS, ALASKAN BROWN BEARS ARE TRULY AWESOME.

Bears are very smart. They have been known to out-wit trappers by rolling rocks into traps; when the traps snap shut, they eat the bait in safety. If campers hang their food from ropes to keep it out of reach of bears, a clever bear might climb the tree, bite through the rope, and feast on the fallen goodies.

A BLACK BEAR
CROUCHES IN
AUTUMN LEAVES.

(LEFT) GIANT PANDAS SPEND A LOT OF THEIR TIME IN TREES.

(RIGHT) A BLACK BEAR WALKS ON ITS HIND LEGS IN SOUTH DAKOTA.

Because bears can walk short distances on their hind legs, some Native Americans called them "the beast that walks like a man." Others performed rituals to try to turn themselves into bears, or wore bear claws around their necks in hopes of magically gaining bears' superhuman power. Throughout the world, bears have always been a symbol of power and strength.

A grizzly bear once fought a lion before a big audience in Mexico. The bear killed the lion so fast that no one saw what happened.

2 BEARS OF THE WORLD

Most Americans know about black bears, grizzly bears, and polar bears. But there are eight different *species*, or kinds, of bears living in Asia, North America, Europe, and South America. No bears live in Africa, Australia, or Antarctica.

The bear you're most likely to run into in North America is the black bear. The black bear lives in wooded areas in every Canadian province, many U.S. states, and parts of Mexico. Despite the name, black bears are not always black. They come in a rainbow of colors from black to reddish brown (called "cinnamon bears") to light brown to white. But the ones found throughout America in parks, forests,

BLACK BEARS ROAM MANY NORTH AMERICAN PARKS. WHEN CAMPERS DON'T STORE FOOD PROPERLY, BEARS MAY COME INTO CAMPSITES AND STEAL IT.

POLAR BEARS LIVE IN THE ICY ARCTIC.

berry-filled meadows—and sometimes even back-yards—are usually black or brown.

The world's most common bear is the brown bear, which lives in mountain forests and river valleys in Europe, Asia, and western North America. Many still live in Canada and Alaska, but very few remain in the northwestern United States. The largest brown bears are two to three times as big as black bears. They also come

14

in a range of colors including black, red, blond, and cinnamon. The best-known brown bear is the grizzly, whose gray-tipped brown fur looks grizzled.

The world's largest bear, the polar bear, lives near the North Pole. These powerful hunters wander hundreds of miles across the arctic ice each year. They have long necks, small heads, and white fur to help them hide in the snow. Their front paws are partially webbed, and they can swim fifty to one hundred miles in

THIS SPECTACLED BEAR IS AT HOME IN THE ANDES MOUNTAINS.

THESE SUN BEARS ARE PLAY-FIGHTING AT A ZOO IN MIAMI.

freezing water. A two-to-four-inch (5–10 cm) layer of fat works like insulation to keep them warm.

One of the world's best-loved bears is the roly-poly giant panda, which has a round, white head, black eye patches, and Mickey Mouse-like ears. These rare creatures live in the mountains of China. Sloth bears, which live in the forests of India and Sri Lanka, have the longest fur of any bear. It is so shaggy that the babies

16

grab hold of it to ride on their mother's backs.

Many bears are named for their markings. The Asiatic black bear, or moon bear, which lives in the Himalayas in Asia, has a white *crescent* moon on its chest. Spectacled bears have white rings around their eyes that look like glasses, or *spectacles.* They live in the Andes of South America and spend most of their time in trees.

Sun bears live in southeast Asian forests and have a white or yellow patch on their necks. Though they look cute, pound for pound they are the most dangerous bear. When bitten by another animal, the sun bear can twist in its loose skin and bite right back.

Except for mothers with young cubs, adult bears usually live alone. Bears can adapt to many environments, but because people have taken over almost all the open spaces, most bears now live in remote forests and mountainsides.

A polar bear can smell a seal from miles away, or through two feet of solid snow.

BEAR SPECIES

The eight species of bears are shown below along with average sizes of the adults. Length is nose to tail.

BROWN BEAR
9 feet (2.7 m)
425 pounds (192.8 kg)

POLAR BEAR
8.5 feet (2.6 m)
700 pounds (317.5 kg)

GIANT PANDA
6 feet (1.8 m)
250 pounds (113 kg)

AMERICAN BLACK BEAR
5 feet (1.5 m)
250 pounds (113 kg)

ASIATIC BLACK BEAR (MOON BEAR)
5 feet (1.5 m)
250 pounds (113 kg)

SLOTH BEAR
5 feet (1.5 m)
250 pounds (113 kg)

SPECTACLED BEAR
5 feet (1.5 m)
250 pounds (113 kg)

SUN BEAR
3 feet (0.9 m)
80 pounds (36.3 kg)

THIS IS A BLACK BEAR SKELETON. YOU CAN SEE BY THE BONES OF THE FEET THAT BEARS WALK ON THEIR HEELS, THEN THE SOLES OF THE FEET, IN THE SAME WAY AS PEOPLE DO.

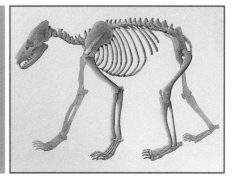

19

3
BEAR NECESSITIES

What do bears eat? Anything they can get their paws on. What food they eat depends on where they live. Some bears eat almost all meat, while others eat only plants and insects.

In Japan brown bears dine mostly on fruits, berries, nuts, and insects. In North America they also hunt deer, moose, beavers, crabs and shellfish. Brown bears love fish. At one waterfall in Alaska where salmon swim up the river each year, sixty–eight bears were seen enjoying the feast at the same time—an amazing sight for these normally lone animals.

Since no plants grow in solid ice, polar bears eat mostly seals and walruses. A swimming polar bear can jump eight feet (2.4 m) out of the water to surprise a snoozing seal. Polar bears will sit for hours by a hole in

A GRIZZLY CUB MUNCHES ON FLOWERS IN A SUMMER MEADOW.

the ice, waiting for a seal to come up for air. When it does—chomp! Because they eat one big meal every four or five days with nothing in between, their stomachs can hold 150 pounds (68 kg) of meat.

Giant pandas are famously finicky eaters. Their diet is limited to a single plant: bamboo, taking in over forty-five pounds (20.4 kg) of the stuff each day. They even have an extra "thumb" on their wrist just for holding bamboo stalks.

Sloth bears' favorite food is termites. They stick their long snouts into termite nests and suck out the insects like a vacuum cleaner. They have no front teeth to slow the slurping and can seal their nostrils for better suction. When they can't get termites, sloth bears climb trees in search of fruit, berries, and honey.

Bears have been known to eat almost anything, including snowmobile seats, engine oil, and rubber boots.

THESE GRIZZLY BEARS ARE SEARCHING FOR BERRIES—A FAVORITE TREAT OF BROWN BEARS EVERYWHERE.

Spectacled bears eat fruit, sugarcane, and corn, which makes them pests to farmers. For meat, they snatch birds, mice, rabbits, and ants or raid cattle and llama ranches. They can also be found in the treetops looking for palm nuts, leaves, and flowers.

FISH, ESPECIALLY SALMON, ARE PART OF THE DIET OF MANY BEARS. HERE A BROWN BEAR CATCHES ONE AS IT SWIMS UPSTREAM IN BROOKS FALLS, ALASKA.

HABITATS THEN & NOW

These maps show the shrinking size of bear habitats.

American black bears and brown bears are both at risk. Areas that once supported a large number of bears now have only small, scattered populations.

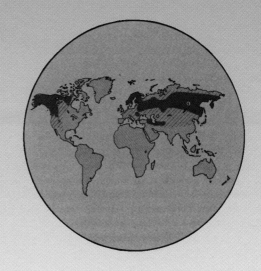

AMERICAN BLACK BEAR

 SCATTERED POPULATION

 LARGE POPULATION

BROWN BEAR

 SCATTERED POPULATION

 LARGE POPULATION

THIS POLAR BEAR HAS DRAGGED ITS KILL, A BEARDED SEAL, ACROSS AN ICEBERG TO EAT.

Sun bears also like trees, devouring the hearts of coconut palms along with lizards, birds, worms, and insects. Sun bears are also called honey bears because they love honey so much. They will endure dozens of stings from angry bees to get to the sticky stuff. And they don't stop there—they eat the bees, too.

The Asiatic black bear angers farmers by killing sheep, goats, and cattle and eating grain from the fields.

Some American black bears have learned to steal campers' food, but mostly they eat berries, bark, grass, and acorns, along with some fish, insects, and dead animals.

Whether they live in forests, mountains, swamps, fields, or on frozen seas, bears somehow always find plenty to eat. They have to—fattening up in the summer is how they get through the winter.

GIANT PANDAS EAT ONLY BAMBOO.

SUN BEARS USE THEIR POWERFUL SENSE OF SMELL TO FIND HONEY.

4
THE BIG SLEEP

Each fall, most bears disappear into caves or dens, where they often stay until spring. Native Americans were amazed that bears could go all winter without eating. Their secret is called *hibernation.*

Hibernation is like sleep, only it lasts for months. When bears hibernate, their heart slows from forty or fifty beats a minute down to just eight, and their temperature drops as much as nine degrees. This uses less energy, which helps bears get through the winter months when there is little to eat.

BEARS, SUCH AS THIS GRIZZLY, SOMETIMES ADD LEAVES TO THEIR DENS TO MAKE THEM WARMER.

ALL BEARS MAKE COZY BEDS WHERE THEY
REST DURING THE DAY. THE NESTS ARE
USUALLY MADE FROM BROKEN BRANCHES,
LEAVES, AND TWIGS, THOUGH POLAR BEARS
SCOOP THEIRS OUT OF THE SNOW. BLACK
BEARS, SUN BEARS, SLOTH BEARS, AND
SPECTACLED BEARS ACTUALLY BUILD THEIR
NESTS IN TREES, AND SOMETIMES EVEN
GIVE BIRTH IN THEM.

The farther north black bears live, the longer their winter hibernation. In Alaska, they may spend up to seven months in their dens to escape the cold. In Mexico black bears may snooze just a few weeks.

(OPPOSITE TOP) ALTHOUGH THEY DO NOT HIBERNATE, POLAR BEARS SLEEP SHORT PERIODS IN DENS. THIS POLAR BEAR DEN IS IN CHURCHILL, CANADA.
(OPPOSITE BOTTOM) TEN DAYS AFTER THEY ARE BORN, GRIZZLY BEAR CUBS ARE STILL VERY SMALL. THIS CUB HAS NOT EVEN OPENED ITS EYES YET.

In order to sleep that long without eating, bears must spend all summer fattening up. In the summer a brown bear may eat eighty pounds (36 kg) of food and put on three to six pounds (2–3 kg) of fat in a single day.

Not all bears hibernate. Polar bears keep on hunting

all winter. Bears that live where plants grow year-round, like sun and sloth bears, stay awake and eat year-round. But even if they don't hibernate, females still go into a den to have their babies.

Bear cubs are blind at birth and weigh less than one pound—small enough to hold in your hand. The tiny cubs stay in the den for a few months, drinking their mothers' milk and growing in safety. When they do come out, they stick close to their mothers for two or three years before going off on their own.

WHEN THEY REACH TWO TO THREE MONTHS, BEAR CUBS VENTURE OUT ON THEIR OWN. HERE ARE THREE BLACK BEAR CUBS.

When male bears grow old enough, they wrestle and fight to compete for the chance to mate. That way, only the strongest bears will have cubs —chances are their young will be strong, too.

Female bears get no help from the males in raising their cubs. In fact, older males sometimes kill and eat bear cubs. This is one of the biggest threats young bears face. But all bears face an even bigger threat from a much more dangerous foe: people.

DURING MATING SEASON, MALE BEARS WILL FIGHT FOR THE CHANCE TO MATE WITH A FEMALE. HERE, TWO POLAR BEARS TUSSLE.

5
BEARS VS. HUMANS

In the past, bears were a threat to people and farm animals. In some places, this is still true. But in most places, it is the bears who are losing the battle for survival.

Most areas in the United States and Europe were cleared of bears long ago. Brown bears are mostly gone from the United States, but many still live in northern Canada and Alaska. Just a few decades ago, the government still killed Alaskan brown bears to help cattle ranchers. But now they are protected, partly because each

TOURISTS COME FROM ALL OVER THE WORLD TO PHOTOGRAPH BEARS IN ALASKA.

37

bear brings about $10,000 a year from tourists who come to take pictures. The cold, northern reaches of the Arctic have yet to attract very many human settlers, so polar bears are less threatened.

But other bears are not so lucky. As people move into remote areas, they are taking many bears' last remaining habitat. Giant pandas are in danger of becoming extinct. Only about one thousand remain in scattered bamboo groves surrounded by people. When the bamboo dies, they have nowhere to go.

BEAR TRAPS, SUCH AS THIS ONE, ARE STILL USED TO CATCH BEARS.

THE FUTURE OF GIANT PANDAS IS AT RISK. IF LAND FOR THEM AND THEIR FOOD SOURCE, BAMBOO, IS NOT SAVED, THEY WILL BECOME EXTINCT.

· · ·

BLACK BEARS IN WASHINGTON EAT A LOT OF TREE BARK. ONE BEAR MIGHT KILL AS MANY AS FIFTY TREES A NIGHT. LUMBER COMPANIES FELT THEY HAD NO CHOICE BUT TO KILL THE HUNGRY BEARS. FINALLY, SOMEONE HAD A BETTER IDEA. WHY NOT JUST LEAVE PILES OF FOOD IN THE FOREST? THE BEARS WERE DELIGHTED AT THE FREE MEALS AND STOPPED EATING THE TREES. SINCE FEEDING THE BEARS COST LESS THAN KILLING THEM, THE LUMBER COMPANIES WERE HAPPY TOO.

· · ·

MOON BEARS ARE OFTEN CAPTURED SO THAT PEOPLE CAN USE THEIR BONES IN TRADITIONAL MEDICINES.

The average life span for bears ranges from twenty-five years for a black bear to twenty-eight years for a polar bear, but bears can live into their forties. The record is a brown bear who lived forty-seven years.

Conservation groups like the World Wildlife Fund are helping make pathways for giant pandas to go safely from one bamboo grove to the next and avoid starvation.

Pandas are not the only bears in danger. Spectacled bears have been pushed into ever more remote mountain areas in South America as farmers move onto the lower slopes. Hungry bears are often killed for eating the farmers' livestock. Sloth bears and moon bears also suffer dwindling numbers as their habitats shrink. Sun bears are so rare that there are now less than one thousand alive.

Another problem is that in many parts of the world, bear parts are used as magic charms or medicines. Thousands of bears are killed just for their gall bladders and paws, which are considered delicacies. Others are captured to perform in circuses.

For wild bears to survive, they will need help from people. Conservationists are fighting to make sure land is set aside for bears before it is too late. Otherwise, several bear species may vanish from the earth forever.

OF THE DIFFERENT KINDS OF BLACK BEARS, IT IS THE LOUISIANA BLACK BEAR AND THE FLORIDA BLACK BEAR THAT ARE IN DANGER OF BECOMING EXTINCT. HABITAT LOSS IS A LARGE PART OF THE PROBLEM. WE CAN ONLY SAVE ANIMALS SUCH AS THIS BLACK BEAR CUB BY PRESERVING THEIR LAND.

Arctic: The cold, icy region near the north pole.

conservationist: A person who works to save, or conserve, wild animals and wild places.

crescent: The narrow, curved shape of the moon when it is lit from the side.

cub: A young bear.

den: A cave found or made by a bear by digging under rocks or fallen logs, for example.

extinct: Gone from the earth forever because every single animal or plant of its kind is dead.

environment: The natural world in which we live.

habitat: The preferred place for an animal species to live.

hibernation: A state of rest much deeper than regular sleep that allows an animal to live on stored fat without eating, drinking, or urinating for several months.

species: A group of animals that are all of the same kind and can produce offspring.

spectacles: Eyeglasses.

ton: Two thousand pounds.

F I N D   O U T   M O R E

BOOKS

Dudley, Karen. *Giant Pandas.* Austin, TX: Raintree Steck–Vaughn, 1997.

Fair, Jeff. *Bears for Kids.* Minnetonka, MN: NorthWord Press, 1991.

Greenaway, Theresa. *Amazing Bears.* NY: Knopf, 1992.

Lynch, Wayne. *Bears, Bears, Bears.* Willowdale, Ontario: Firefly Books, 1995.

Pettersson, Bertil. *In the Bears' Forest.* NY: Farrar, Straus, and Giroux, 1991.

Stirling, Ian. *Bears.* San Francisco: Sierra Club Books for Children, 1992.

Tracqui, Valerie. *The Brown Bear: Giant of the Mountains.* Watertown, MA: Charlesbridge, 1998.

WEBSITES

North American Bear Center

http://www.bear.org

The Bear Den/The Cub Den

http://www.nature–net.com/bears

The Bear Den (American Zoo and Aquarium Association)

http://www.bearden.org

Bears.org

http://www.bears.org

Martin Schwabacher grew up in Minneapolis, Minnesota, and has lived in Rhode Island, Texas, and New York City. He is the author of more than fifteen books for young people, including *Elephants* in the Animals Animals series.